Mastering Laravel

Preface

Laravel is a powerful and elegant PHP framework that has become the go-to choice for building web applications. Its simplicity, flexibility, and ease of use have made it the preferred choice for both beginners and experienced developers.

This book is a comprehensive guide to Laravel, covering all the essential topics that you need to know to build modern web applications. Whether you are a beginner or an experienced developer, this book has something to offer.

The book covers the basics of Laravel, such as installation, configuration, and routing. It also delves into more advanced topics, such as middleware, authentication, authorization, and API development.

The book also covers important topics related to deployment and maintenance, including version control, automated testing, error handling, security, and performance optimization. Additionally, it includes a chapter on deploying Laravel applications with Docker, which is becoming an increasingly popular option for deploying web applications.

Throughout the book, you will learn by building real-world applications, with examples and code snippets provided to help you follow along. The book also includes additional resources, such as recommended books and articles, to help you further your learning.

By the end of this book, you will have a solid understanding of Laravel and the tools and techniques needed to build robust and scalable web applications.

Note! Every effort has been made to present the information as up-to-date and error-free as possible. Due to (future) updates, it is possible that the information no longer corresponds completely with the then usual version of Laravel.

A. Scholtens

Table of Contents

Chapter 1: Introduction

Laravel is a popular open-source PHP framework used for web application development. It is known for its elegant syntax, modular structure, and robust features, which make it easy to build scalable and maintainable web applications. This chapter will introduce you to Laravel, how to install it, and how to create a new Laravel project.

1.1 Introduction to Laravel

Laravel was created by Taylor Otwell in 2011 and has since become one of the most widely used PHP frameworks worldwide. It follows the Model-View-Controller (MVC) architecture, making it easy to separate application logic, presentation, and data storage. Laravel comes with a wide range of features that make web development fast and efficient, including routing, templating, middleware, and authentication.

1.2 Installing Laravel

To install Laravel, you need to have PHP, Composer, and a web server installed on your machine. Composer is a PHP dependency manager that manages Laravel's dependencies and packages. Here are the steps to install Laravel using Composer:

> Step 1: Install Composer First, you need to download and install Composer from the official website (https://getcomposer.org/).

Composer is available for Windows, Mac, and Linux operating systems.

Step 2: Install Laravel Once you have installed Composer, open your terminal or command prompt and run the following command:

```
composer global require laravel/installer
```

This will install the Laravel installer globally on your system, making it available for use in any directory.

1.3 Creating a new Laravel project

After installing Laravel, you can create a new Laravel project using the following steps:

Step 1: Create a new project directory Open your terminal or command prompt and create a new directory for your Laravel project:

```
mkdir myproject
```

Step 2: Navigate to the project directory Navigate to the project directory you just created:

```
cd myproject
```

Step 3: Create a new Laravel project Run the following command to create a new Laravel project:

laravel new myproject

This will create a new Laravel project named 'myproject' in the current directory. It will take a few minutes to install all the required dependencies and packages.

Step 4: Serve the Laravel project Once the installation is complete, you can start the development server using the following command:

php artisan serve

This will start the development server on port 8000. You can now open your web browser and navigate to http://localhost:8000 to see the Laravel welcome page.

Chapter summary

In this chapter, we have introduced you to Laravel, its features, and how to install it. We have also covered how to create a new Laravel project using the Laravel installer. With Laravel installed and a new project created, you are now ready to start building your web application. In the next chapter, we will dive deeper into Laravel's MVC architecture and how to create routes and controllers for your application.

Chapter 2: Laravel Basics

In this chapter, we will cover the basics of Laravel, including its Model-View-Controller (MVC) architecture, how to create routes and controllers, views and Blade templating, and models and Eloquent ORM.

Understanding MVC architecture: Laravel follows the MVC architecture pattern, which separates application logic, presentation, and data storage. The MVC architecture comprises three components:

1. Model: Represents the data and business logic of the application.

2. View: Represents the presentation layer of the application.

3. Controller: Handles the user input and updates the model and view accordingly.

Routes and Controllers: Routes and controllers are essential components of the Laravel framework. Routes define the URL endpoints of your application, and controllers handle the logic associated with each route.

Routes are defined in the **'routes/web.php'** file. Here's an example of a route definition:

```
Route::get('/users', 'UserController@index');
```

In this example, we define a **'GET'** route for the **'/users'** endpoint. When this route is accessed, the **'index'** method of the **'UserController'** class will be called.

Controllers are defined in the **'app/Http/Controllers'** directory. Here's an example of a controller:

```php
<?php

namespace App\Http\Controllers;

use Illuminate\Http\Request;

class UserController extends Controller
{
    public function index()
    {
        // Logic to fetch all users
        return view('users.index');
    }
}
```

In this example, we define a **'UserController'** class with an **'index'** method. The **'index'** method fetches all users and returns a view named **'users.index'**.

Views and Blade Templating: Views are responsible for rendering the presentation layer of your application. In Laravel, views are typically written using Blade templating, which provides a simple and powerful syntax for defining your application's HTML.

Here's an example of a view that displays a list of users:

```html
<!DOCTYPE html>
<html>
  <head>
    <title>Users</title>
  </head>
  <body>
    <h1>Users</h1>
    <ul>
      @foreach ($users as $user)
        <li>{{ $user->name }}</li>
      @endforeach
    </ul>
  </body>
</html>
```

In this example, we define an HTML view that displays a list of users using the '**@foreach**' directive. The '**{{ $user->name }}**' expression is used to output the name of each user in the list.

Models and Eloquent ORM: Models represent the data and business logic of your application. In Laravel, models are typically created using Eloquent ORM, which provides a simple and powerful way to interact with your application's database.

Here's an example of a model that represents a User:

```php
<?php

namespace App\Models;

use Illuminate\Database\Eloquent\Model;
class User extends Model
{
    protected $fillable = [
        'name',
        'email',
        'password',
    ];
}
```

In this example, we define a **'User'** model that extends the **'Illuminate\Database\Eloquent\Model'** class. The **'$fillable'** property is used to specify which attributes can be mass-assigned.

Chapter summary

In this chapter, we covered the basics of Laravel, including its MVC architecture, routes and controllers, views and Blade templating, and models and Eloquent ORM. By understanding these fundamental concepts, you can start building your Laravel application and take advantage of the framework's powerful features. In the next chapter, we will dive deeper into controllers and middleware and how to handle HTTP requests and responses.

Chapter 3: Database Management

In this chapter, we will cover the database management features of Laravel, including how to set up and configure your database, create database migrations and seed data, and query data using the Eloquent ORM.

Database setup and configuration: Laravel supports several types of databases, including MySQL, PostgreSQL, SQLite, and SQL Server. To set up and configure your database, you will need to edit the '**.env**' file in the root directory of your Laravel project.

Here's an example of a MySQL database configuration:

```
DB_CONNECTION=mysql
DB_HOST=127.0.0.1
DB_PORT=3306
DB_DATABASE=myapp
DB_USERNAME=root
DB_PASSWORD=
```

In this example, we define the database connection as MySQL and specify the database host, port, name, username, and password.

Database migrations and seeding: Database migrations allow you to define changes to your database schema in code, making it easy to manage changes across multiple environments.

To create a new migration, you can use the **'make:migration'** Artisan command:

    php artisan make:migration create_users_table --create=users

In this example, we create a new migration named **'create_users_table'** and specify that it will create a new **'users'** table.

Once you have defined your migrations, you can use the **'migrate'** Artisan command to run them:

    php artisan migrate

Database seeding allows you to populate your database with sample data for testing and development purposes. To create a new seeder, you can use the **'make:seeder'** Artisan command:

    php artisan make:seeder UsersTableSeeder

In this example, we create a new seeder named **'UsersTableSeeder'**. To run the seeder, you can use the **'db:seed'** Artisan command:

    php artisan db:seed --class=UsersTableSeeder

Querying data using Eloquent ORM: Eloquent ORM provides a simple and powerful way to interact with your database using PHP. To use Eloquent, you will need to define a model for each table in your database.

Here's an example of a User model:

```php
<?php

namespace App\Models;

use Illuminate\Database\Eloquent\Model;

class User extends Model
{
    protected $fillable = [
        'name',
        'email',
        'password',
    ];
}
```

In this example, we define a **'User'** model with the **'$fillable'** property that specifies which attributes can be mass-assigned.

To query data using Eloquent, you can use methods such as **'all'**, **'find'**, **'where'**, and **'orderBy'**. Here's an example of querying all users:

```php
$users = User::all();
```

In this example, we use the **'all'** method to fetch all users from the **'users'** table. You can also chain additional methods to filter and sort the results:

```
$users = User::where('active', true)
        ->orderBy('name', 'asc')
        ->get();
```

Chapter summary

In this chapter, we covered the database management features of Laravel, including how to set up and configure your database, create database migrations and seed data, and query data using the Eloquent ORM. By understanding these features, you can efficiently manage your application's database and interact with it using Eloquent ORM. In the next chapter, we will cover middleware and how to handle HTTP requests and responses.

Chapter 4: Form Handling and Validation

In this chapter, we will cover how to handle form submissions, validate form data using Laravel's built-in validators, and display form errors to the user.

Handling Form Submissions When a user submits a form, the form data is typically sent to the server using an HTTP POST request. In Laravel, you can handle form submissions using a controller method. Here's an example:

```php
public function handleContactForm(Request $request)
{
    // handle form submission
}
```

In this example, we define a **'handleContactForm'** method that takes a **'Request'** object as its argument. The **'Request'** object contains the form data submitted by the user.

Validating Form Data Using Laravel's Built-in Validators To ensure that the form data submitted by the user is valid, we need to validate it. Laravel provides several built-in validators that we can use to validate form data. Here's an example of how to use the **'required'** validator to validate that a form field is not empty:

```php
public function handleContactForm(Request $request)
{
    $validatedData = $request->validate([
        'name' => 'required',
```

```
        'email' => 'required|email',
        'message' => 'required',
    ]);


    // handle form submission
}
```

In this example, we use the **'validate'** method on the **'Request'** object to validate the form data. The **'validate'** method takes an array of validation rules, where the keys are the names of the form fields and the values are the validation rules.

In this case, we have three validation rules:

- **'name'** is required
- **'email'** is required and must be a valid email address
- **'message'** is required

If the validation fails, Laravel will automatically redirect the user back to the form page and display the validation errors.

Displaying Form Errors When the user submits a form that fails validation, we need to display the validation errors to the user so that they can correct their mistakes. In Laravel, we can display the validation errors using Blade templates.

Here's an example:

```
<form action="/contact" method="POST">
  @csrf

  <div class="form-group">
    <label for="name">Name</label>
    <input type="text" name="name" id="name" value="{{ old('name') }}" class="form-control{{ $errors->has('name') ? ' is-invalid' : '' }}">

    @if ($errors->has('name'))
      <div class="invalid-feedback">{{ $errors->first('name') }}</div>
    @endif
  </div>

  <!-- more form fields -->

  <button type="submit" class="btn btn-primary">Submit</button>
</form>
```

In this example, we use Blade's **'old'** function to pre-fill the form fields with the old input values. We also use the **'has'** method on the **'$errors'** object to check if there are any validation errors for a particular form field.
If there are validation errors, we add the **'is-invalid'** class to the form field and display the error message using the **'$errors->first'** method.

Chapter summary

In this chapter, we covered how to handle form submissions, validate form data using Laravel's built-in validators, and display form errors to the user. By understanding these features, you can create robust and user-friendly forms in your Laravel application. In the next chapter, we will cover authentication and authorization, including how to handle user login and registration.

Chapter 5: User Authentication

In this chapter, we will cover how to implement user authentication and registration in Laravel, including password reset functionality and user roles and permissions.

User Authentication and Registration Laravel provides built-in authentication functionality that allows you to easily implement user authentication and registration. To get started, you can use the **'make:auth'** Artisan command to generate the authentication scaffolding:

```
php artisan make:auth
```

This command will generate the necessary views and routes for user authentication and registration.

You can also customize the authentication views by running the **'php artisan vendor:publish --tag=laravel-views'** command. This will copy the default authentication views to the **'resources/views/vendor'** directory, where you can customize them as needed.

Password Reset Functionality Laravel also provides built-in password reset functionality. To enable this feature, you need to ensure that your user model implements the

'Illuminate\Contracts\Auth\CanResetPassword' interface and uses the **'Illuminate\Auth\Passwords\CanResetPassword'** trait. Here's an example:

```
use Illuminate\Contracts\Auth\CanResetPassword;
use Illuminate\Auth\Passwords\CanResetPassword as
CanResetPasswordTrait;

class User extends Authenticatable implements CanResetPassword
{
    use CanResetPasswordTrait;

    // ...
}
```

Once you have set up your user model, you can use the **'php artisan make:auth'** command to generate the necessary views and routes for password reset functionality.

User Roles and Permissions In some applications, you may need to assign different roles and permissions to your users. Laravel provides a powerful authorization system that allows you to define roles and permissions and control access to different parts of your application.

To get started, you can use the **'make:policy'** Artisan command to generate a policy for a specific model:

```
php artisan make:policy PostPolicy --model=Post
```

In this example, we generate a **'PostPolicy'** policy for the **'Post'** model. The policy defines the rules for accessing the model's resources.

You can also use the **'authorize'** method in your controllers to check if a user has the necessary permissions to access a resource. Here's an example:

```php
public function update(Request $request, Post $post)
{
    $this->authorize('update', $post);


    // update the post
}
```

In this example, we use the **'authorize'** method to check if the user has the **'update'** permission for the specified **'Post'** model. If the user does not have the necessary permission, Laravel will automatically return a 403 Forbidden HTTP response.

Chapter summary

In this chapter, we covered how to implement user authentication and registration in Laravel, including password reset functionality and user roles and permissions. By understanding these features, you can create secure and flexible user management systems in your Laravel application. In the next chapter, we will cover how to use Laravel's built-in email sending functionality.

Chapter 6: Security and Middleware

In this chapter, we will cover how to implement security measures in your Laravel application using middleware. We will cover CSRF protection, authentication middleware, and authorization middleware.

Understanding Middleware in Laravel Middleware is a powerful feature in Laravel that allows you to intercept and modify incoming HTTP requests. Middleware functions like a filter that sits between the client and the application, and can be used to perform tasks such as authentication, validation, and logging.

Laravel comes with several built-in middleware that you can use out of the box, or you can create your own custom middleware.

To create a middleware, you can use the **'make:middleware'** Artisan command:

    php artisan make:middleware MyMiddleware

This will create a new middleware class in the **'app/Http/Middleware'** directory.

To apply middleware to your routes, you can use the **'middleware'** method in your route definitions:

    Route::get('/dashboard', 'DashboardController@index')
    ->middleware('auth');

In this example, we apply the **'auth'** middleware to the **'/dashboard'** route, which ensures that the user is authenticated before accessing the dashboard.

CSRF Protection Cross-Site Request Forgery (CSRF) is a common security vulnerability that can allow an attacker to perform actions on behalf of a user without their knowledge or consent. Laravel provides built-in CSRF protection middleware that helps protect your application against this type of attack.

To enable CSRF protection, you can apply the **'web'** middleware group to your routes:

```
Route::group(['middleware' => ['web']], function () {
    // your routes here
});
```

This middleware group includes the **'VerifyCsrfToken'** middleware, which checks for a valid CSRF token on all incoming POST, PUT, and DELETE requests.

Authentication Middleware Authentication middleware is used to ensure that a user is logged in before accessing protected parts of your application. Laravel provides built-in authentication middleware that you can use to secure your routes.

To apply authentication middleware to your routes, you can use the **'auth'** middleware:

```
Route::get('/dashboard', 'DashboardController@index')
->middleware('auth');
```

Note for the reader: the parts must be fed in together, so
Route::get('/dashboard', 'DashboardController@index')->middleware('auth');
this also applies to the other codes later in this chapter

This will ensure that the user is authenticated before accessing the dashboard.

You can also use the **'guest'** middleware to protect routes that should only be accessible to guests (i.e., users who are not logged in):

```
Route::get('/login', 'Auth\LoginController@showLoginForm')
->middleware('guest');
```

Authorization Middleware Authorization middleware is used to control access to resources based on a user's permissions. Laravel provides built-in authorization middleware that you can use to protect your routes.

To apply authorization middleware to your routes, you can use the **'can'** middleware:

```
Route::get('/dashboard', 'DashboardController@index')
->middleware('can:view-dashboard');
```

In this example, we apply the **'can:view-dashboard'** middleware, which checks if the user has the **'view-dashboard'** permission before allowing them to access the dashboard.

You can define your own permissions and policies using Laravel's built-in authorization system. To create a new policy, you can use the **'make:policy'** Artisan command:

```
php artisan make:policy PostPolicy --model=Post
```

This will generate a new policy class in the **'app/Policies'** directory, which you can use to define the rules for accessing your resources.

Chapter summary

In this chapter, we covered how to implement security measures in your Laravel application using middleware. We covered CSRF protection, authentication middleware, and authorization middleware, and explained how to create your own custom middleware and policies. By understanding these security features, you can create a robust and secure application in Laravel. In the next chapter, we will cover how to work with files and uploads in Laravel and explore various techniques to handle file uploads, validate file types and sizes, and store files in the filesystem or cloud storage.

Chapter 7: File Handling and Uploads

In this chapter, we will cover how to handle files and uploads in your Laravel application. We will discuss how to upload files, validate file types and sizes, and store files in the filesystem or cloud storage.

Uploading Files Laravel provides a simple and convenient way to handle file uploads using the **'Illuminate\Http\UploadedFile'** class. This class represents an uploaded file and provides methods for working with the file's properties and contents.

To upload a file, you can create a form with an input field of type **'file'**:

```
<form method="POST" action="/upload" enctype="multipart/form-data">
    @csrf
    <input type="file" name="file">
    <button type="submit">Upload</button>
</form>
```

In this example, we create a form with a file input field and use the **'enctype="multipart/form-data" '** attribute to indicate that we are uploading files.

In your controller, you can handle the file upload by calling the **'store'** method on the uploaded file:

```php
public function upload(Request $request)
{

        $file = $request->file('file');
        $path = $file->store('uploads');
        return "File uploaded to: $path";

}
```

In this example, we get the uploaded file from the request using the **'file'** method, and then call the **'store'** method to store the file in the **'storage/app/uploads'** directory. The **'store'** method automatically generates a unique filename for the uploaded file and returns the path to the stored file.

Validating Files When uploading files, it is important to validate the file type and size to prevent malicious or invalid files from being uploaded to your application. Laravel provides several built-in validators that you can use to validate files.

To validate the file type, you can use the **'mimes'** validator:

```php
$request->validate([
        'file' => 'required|file|mimes:jpg,png,gif',
]);
```

In this example, we use the **'mimes'** validator to ensure that the uploaded file is a JPG, PNG, or GIF image.

To validate the file size, you can use the **'max'** validator:

```php
$request->validate([
    'file' => 'required|file|max:1024',
]);
```

In this example, we use the **'max'** validator to ensure that the uploaded file is no larger than 1MB.

Storing Files Laravel provides several drivers for storing files, including the local filesystem, Amazon S3, and Rackspace Cloud Files. To configure your filesystem, you can use the **'config/filesystems.php'** configuration file.

To store files in the local filesystem, you can use the **'store'** method with the **'local'** driver:

```php
$path = $file->store('uploads', 'local');
```

In this example, we store the file in the **'uploads'** directory using the **'local'** driver.

To store files in cloud storage, you can use the **'store'** method with the appropriate driver:

```php
$path = $file->store('uploads', 's3');
```

In this example, we store the file in the **'uploads'** directory using the Amazon S3 driver.

Chapter summary

In this chapter, we covered how to handle files and uploads in your Laravel application. We discussed how to upload files, validate file types and sizes, and store files in the filesystem or cloud storage. By understanding these file handling features, you can create a robust and efficient file upload system in Laravel. In the next chapter, we will cover how to work with email in Laravel.

Chapter 8: Security and middleware

Security and middleware are critical aspects of any web application, including those built on Laravel. Middleware in Laravel is a way of filtering HTTP requests and responses to your application. It acts as a bridge between the client and the server, intercepting and modifying requests and responses as necessary. In this chapter, we'll cover some of the essential middleware and security features that are included in Laravel.

8.1 Understanding Middleware in Laravel

Middleware can be thought of as a series of filters that execute before or after a request is handled by your application. Middleware can be used for various purposes, such as authentication, logging, and routing. In Laravel, middleware can be defined either globally or locally. Global middleware applies to all routes in your application, while local middleware is applied to specific routes or groups of routes.

To define a middleware class in Laravel, you can use the **'make:middleware'** Artisan command. This command will generate a new middleware class in the **'app/Http/Middleware'** directory. The middleware class will have a **'handle'** method, which is where you define the logic for the middleware.

8.2 CSRF Protection

Cross-Site Request Forgery (CSRF) is an attack that exploits the trust that a website has in a user's browser. It involves tricking a user into executing an action on a website without their knowledge or consent. Laravel provides built-in CSRF protection to prevent these types of attacks.

When a user submits a form in Laravel, a CSRF token is generated and added to the form as a hidden input. When the form is submitted, Laravel verifies that the token in the request matches the one that was generated. If the tokens don't match, the request is rejected.

To enable CSRF protection in Laravel, you can include the **'csrf'** middleware in the global middleware stack. This middleware is included by default in Laravel's **'web'** middleware group, which is applied to all web routes. You can also add the **'@csrf'** Blade directive to your forms to automatically include the CSRF token.

8.3 Authentication Middleware

Authentication is the process of verifying that a user is who they claim to be. In Laravel, authentication middleware is used to restrict access to certain routes or controllers based on whether the user is authenticated.

Laravel provides built-in authentication middleware that can be applied to routes or controllers. The **'auth'** middleware restricts access to authenticated users, while the **'guest'** middleware restricts access to unauthenticated users. You can apply these middleware to your routes or controllers using the **'middleware'** method or by adding them to your route groups.

8.4 Authorization Middleware

Authorization is the process of determining whether a user has the necessary permissions to perform a certain action. In Laravel, authorization middleware is used to restrict access to certain routes or controllers based on the user's permissions.

Laravel provides built-in authorization middleware that can be used to check a user's permissions. The **'can'** middleware allows you to specify a policy or callback that will be used to check the user's permissions. You can apply this middleware to your routes or controllers using the **'middleware'** method or by adding it to your route groups.

Chapter summary

Middleware and security features are essential components of any Laravel application. Middleware can be used for various purposes, such as authentication, logging, and routing. Laravel provides built-in middleware for CSRF protection, authentication, and authorization, which can be applied to your routes or controllers as needed. By understanding and using these features, you can create a robust and secure application in Laravel.

Chapter 9: API Development

API (Application Programming Interface) development has become an essential part of web development, enabling applications to communicate with each other and exchange data. Laravel provides a convenient and powerful way to build APIs using its built-in functionality. In this chapter, we'll cover the basics of building APIs with Laravel, RESTful API design principles, and how to document your API using Swagger/OpenAPI.

9.1 Building APIs with Laravel

Laravel provides a convenient way to build APIs using its built-in routing and controller functionality. To create an API endpoint in Laravel, you can define a route in your **'api.php'** file and map it to a controller method that handles the request.

```
Route::get('/users', 'UserController@index');
```

In this example, we're defining a route for the **'/users'** endpoint, which maps to the **'index'** method of the **'UserController'**. The **'index'** method can return a JSON response, which can be consumed by other applications.

Laravel's routing system makes it easy to handle various HTTP verbs for performing CRUD operations on resources. For example, a **'GET'** request can be used to retrieve a resource, while a **'POST'** request can be used to create a new resource. Similarly, a **'PUT'** request can be used to update an existing resource, while a **'DELETE'** request can be used to remove a resource.

Laravel's routing system allows developers to map HTTP requests to specific controller methods that handle the request. This makes it easy to implement RESTful API endpoints that adhere to the CRUD principles.

Furthermore, Laravel provides a variety of tools for working with data, including Eloquent ORM for interacting with databases and collections for working with arrays of data. These tools make it easy to build APIs that perform complex operations on data.

In addition to handling HTTP verbs, Laravel's routing system also allows for handling of route parameters and query parameters. This makes it easy to build flexible APIs that can handle a wide range of requests.

Overall, Laravel provides a powerful set of tools for building APIs that are flexible, scalable, and secure. By leveraging Laravel's built-in support for handling HTTP verbs, developers can quickly build APIs that adhere to RESTful design principles and provide a great user experience.

9.2 RESTful API Design Principles

REST (Representational State Transfer) is a set of architectural principles used to design APIs. A RESTful API is designed to be simple, scalable, and easy to use. It uses standard HTTP verbs and status codes to interact with resources.

In a RESTful API, resources are represented by URLs, and HTTP verbs are used to perform CRUD operations on these resources. For example, to retrieve a list of users, you would send a **'GET'** request to the **'/users'** endpoint. To create a new user, you would send a **'POST'** request to the same endpoint.

To design a RESTful API in Laravel, you can follow these principles:

- Use HTTP verbs to perform CRUD operations on resources.

- Use URLs to represent resources.

- Use standard HTTP status codes to indicate the status of a request.

- Use JSON as the data format for responses.

9.3 API Documentation with Swagger/OpenAPI

API documentation is critical for developers who want to consume your API. It provides a reference for the endpoints, parameters, and responses of your API. Swagger/OpenAPI is a specification for documenting RESTful APIs.

Laravel provides built-in support for generating Swagger/OpenAPI documentation for your API using the **'darkaonline/l5-swagger'** package. This package allows you to generate documentation automatically based on your Laravel routes.

To generate Swagger/OpenAPI documentation in Laravel, you can follow these steps:

1. Install the **'darkaonline/l5-swagger'** package using Composer.

2. Publish the Swagger configuration file using the **'php artisan vendor:publish --provider "L5Swagger\L5SwaggerServiceProvider"'** command.

3. Configure the Swagger settings in the **'config/l5-swagger.php'** file.

4. Add Swagger annotations to your controller methods to describe the endpoints and responses.

5. Generate the Swagger documentation using the **'php artisan l5-swagger:generate'** command.

Chapter summary

Building APIs with Laravel is straightforward and convenient, thanks to Laravel's built-in functionality. RESTful API design principles provide a standard way to design APIs that are simple, scalable, and easy to use. API documentation is critical for developers who want to consume your API, and Swagger/OpenAPI is a useful tool for generating documentation automatically.

Chapter 10: Front-end Development

Front-end development is an important aspect of building modern web applications. In this chapter, we will explore how Laravel can be used to build responsive front-end layouts and integrate popular front-end frameworks like Bootstrap.

10.1 Integrating Bootstrap with Laravel

Bootstrap is a popular front-end framework that provides a set of pre-designed components and styles for building responsive web applications. Laravel provides built-in support for integrating Bootstrap into your project.

To get started, you can use Laravel Mix, a wrapper around the popular Webpack module bundler, to compile and bundle your front-end assets. Laravel Mix comes pre-configured with support for compiling CSS and JavaScript, which makes it easy to integrate Bootstrap.

First, you will need to install Bootstrap and its dependencies using npm:

```
npm install bootstrap jquery popper.js
```

Next, you can import the Bootstrap CSS and JavaScript files into your Laravel application by adding the following code to your app.scss file:

```
// Import Bootstrap CSS
@import '~bootstrap/scss/bootstrap';
```

```
// Import Bootstrap JavaScript
import 'bootstrap';
```

You can then compile your assets using Laravel Mix by running the following command:

```
npm run dev
```

Laravel Mix will compile your assets and place them in the public directory of your Laravel project.

10.2 Building responsive front-end layouts with Blade

Blade is Laravel's templating engine that provides an easy way to build reusable front-end components. Blade allows you to write clean and concise templates using simple syntax, while also providing a powerful set of features like conditional rendering and looping.

To get started with Blade, you can create a new Blade template file using the .blade.php extension. In this template file, you can use Blade's syntax to include other templates, render dynamic data, and conditionally render content.

For example, you can use Blade's @if directive to conditionally render content based on a boolean value:

```
@if ($user->isAdmin())
    <p>Welcome, admin!</p>
@else
    <p>Welcome, user!</p>
@endif
```

You can also use Blade's @foreach directive to loop through an array of data and render each item:

```
@foreach ($products as $product)
    <div class="card">
        <h2>{{ $product->name }}</h2>
        <p>{{ $product->description }}</p>
    </div>
@endforeach
```

In addition to Blade's basic features, Laravel also provides a set of Blade directives for working with forms, authentication, and more.

Chapter summary

Overall, Laravel provides a powerful set of tools for building responsive front-end layouts and integrating popular front-end frameworks like Bootstrap. By leveraging Laravel's built-in support for front-end development, you can build modern and responsive web applications with ease.

Chapter 11: Deployment and Maintenance

Deployment and maintenance are critical aspects of building web applications. In this chapter, we will explore best practices for deploying and maintaining Laravel applications.

11.1 Deploying Laravel projects to production servers

Deploying a Laravel project to a production server can be a complex process that requires careful planning and attention to detail. Here are some best practices to follow when deploying a Laravel project:

1. Use a version control system like Git to manage your codebase and track changes.

A version control system (VCS) like Git is an essential tool for managing the codebase of any software project, including Laravel applications. Here are some of the benefits of using a VCS like Git:

I. Version control: Git allows you to keep track of changes to your codebase over time. With Git, you can create branches for new features, bug fixes, and other changes, and then merge them back into the main codebase when they're ready. This allows you to keep track of changes and maintain a history of your codebase.

II. Collaboration: Git makes it easy for multiple developers to work on the same codebase simultaneously. Each developer can create their own branch for their changes and then merge them back into the main codebase when they're ready. This reduces the risk of conflicts and makes it easier to work together on complex projects.

III. Rollbacks: Git allows you to roll back to a previous version of your codebase if something goes wrong. This can be invaluable if you accidentally introduce a bug or if a change causes unexpected issues.

IV. Code reviews: Git makes it easy to review and comment on changes to the codebase. This can help improve code quality and catch issues before they make it into production.

To use Git with your Laravel project, you'll need to set up a Git repository and start committing changes to it. You can use a service like GitHub, GitLab, or Bitbucket to host your repository and collaborate with other developers.

When committing changes to your Git repository, be sure to include a clear and descriptive commit message that explains the changes you made. This can help make it easier to understand what changes were made and why, which can be helpful when reviewing code or debugging issues.

2. Use a deployment tool like Capistrano or Deployer to automate the deployment process and ensure consistency across environments.

Deploying a Laravel application to production can be a complex process, involving a number of steps including running database migrations, clearing caches, and uploading code files. Manually performing these steps can be time-consuming and error-prone, especially as your application grows and you need to deploy to multiple environments.

Using a deployment tool like Capistrano or Deployer can help automate the deployment process and ensure consistency across environments. Here are some of the benefits of using a deployment tool:

I.   Consistency: A deployment tool ensures that the same steps are followed every time you deploy your application, reducing the risk of errors and inconsistencies across environments.

II.   Automation: A deployment tool automates many of the steps involved in deploying an application, saving time and reducing the risk of human error.

III.   Scalability: As your application grows, deploying manually becomes increasingly difficult and time-consuming. A deployment tool can help you scale your deployment process and make it more efficient.

IV.   Rollbacks: A deployment tool can make it easier to roll back to a previous version of your application if something goes wrong during the deployment process.

To use a deployment tool with your Laravel application, you'll need to set up a deployment script that defines the steps to be taken during the deployment process. This might include running database migrations, clearing caches, uploading code files, and restarting servers (for further information and an example of the script, see Appendix A).

Once you have your deployment script set up, you can use the deployment tool to automate the deployment process across multiple environments. This can help ensure consistency and reliability across your development, staging, and production environments.

3. Use environment variables to manage sensitive information like database credentials and API keys.

When building applications, it's common to use sensitive information like database credentials, API keys, and other secrets. It's important to ensure that these sensitive information are not hardcoded in the application code, as this makes them vulnerable to unauthorized access or exposure.

Instead, it's recommended to use environment variables to manage sensitive information. Environment variables are variables that are defined outside of the application code and are accessible within the application. They allow you to store sensitive information securely and make it easy to manage different configurations for different environments.

In Laravel, you can use the '**.env**' file to define environment variables. This file is located in the root directory of your Laravel application and contains key-value pairs of environment variables. For example, to define a database connection, you can add the following to your '**.env**' file:

```
DB_CONNECTION=mysql
DB_HOST=127.0.0.1
DB_PORT=3306
```

```
DB_DATABASE=mydatabase
DB_USERNAME=myusername
DB_PASSWORD=mypassword
```

You can then access these environment variables in your Laravel application using the **env()** function. For example, to retrieve the database connection details, you can use the following code:

```
DB_CONNECTION=mysql
DB_HOST=127.0.0.1
DB_PORT=3306
DB_DATABASE=mydatabase
DB_USERNAME=myusername
DB_PASSWORD=mypassword
```

```php
$connection = env('DB_CONNECTION');
$host = env('DB_HOST');
$port = env('DB_PORT');
$database = env('DB_DATABASE');
$username = env('DB_USERNAME');
$password = env('DB_PASSWORD');

$db = new PDO("{$connection}:host={$host};port={$port};dbname={$database}", $username, $password);
```

By using environment variables, you can easily switch between different configurations for different environments (e.g. development, staging, production) without changing your application code. You can also avoid accidentally exposing sensitive information, as the **'.env'** file can be excluded from version control systems like Git.

4. Set up automated backups to ensure that your data is always safe and secure.

Automated backups are an essential part of any deployment and maintenance process, as they help ensure that your data is always safe and secure. In Laravel, you can use a number of tools and services to set up automated backups for your application.

One popular option is to use a third-party backup service like Backblaze, which offers an automated backup solution for Laravel applications. With Backblaze, you can schedule regular backups of your application's database, files, and other critical data, and store them securely in the cloud.

Another option is to use a backup tool like Laravel Backup, which is a free and open-source package that provides a simple and flexible backup solution for Laravel applications. With Laravel Backup, you can set up automated backups of your application's database and files, and store them on a local or remote server.

To set up automated backups in Laravel, you will first need to configure the backup tool or service you are using to connect to your application's database and file system. This typically involves creating a backup configuration file that specifies the backup frequency, location, and other settings.

Once your backup tool or service is configured, you can then set up a cron job or other scheduled task to run the backup script at regular intervals. This will ensure that your data is backed up automatically on a regular basis, reducing the risk of data loss and making it easier to recover from any unexpected issues or failures.

5. Use a content delivery network (CDN) to speed up the delivery of static assets like images and CSS.

A Content Delivery Network (CDN) is a distributed network of servers that deliver content to end-users based on their geographic location. CDNs are used to speed up the delivery of static assets like images and CSS by caching them on servers closer to the end-users.

In Laravel, using a CDN for static assets is relatively easy. First, you need to choose a CDN provider and sign up for their service. Some popular CDN providers include Cloudflare, Amazon CloudFront, and MaxCDN.

Once you've signed up for a CDN service, you need to configure Laravel to use the CDN for static assets. This is typically done by updating the asset URLs in your application to point to the CDN URL instead of the local URL.

For example, if you have an image at **'public/images/logo.png'**, you would update the HTML code to reference the CDN URL instead of the local URL:

```
<img src="https://cdn.example.com/images/logo.png">
```

You can also use Laravel's built-in asset() function to automatically generate the correct CDN URL based on your configuration. To do this, you'll need to update your **'config/app.php'** file to include your CDN configuration:

```
'cdn' => [
    'url' => 'https://cdn.example.com',
],
```

Then, you can use the **'asset()'** function to generate the CDN URL for your assets:

```
<img src="{{ asset('images/logo.png', true) }}">
```

The second parameter in the **'asset()'** function tells Laravel to use the CDN URL instead of the local URL.

Using a CDN can significantly improve the performance of your Laravel application by reducing the time it takes to load static assets. Additionally, using a CDN can also reduce the load on your server, which can improve the overall reliability of your application.

6. Use a caching layer like Redis or Memcached to improve performance
    and reduce database load.

When building Laravel applications, it's important to consider performance
optimization strategies. One such strategy is to use a caching layer to reduce
database load and improve response times. Laravel makes it easy to
integrate caching services like Redis or Memcached into your application.

Redis and Memcached are both in-memory key-value data stores that allow
you to cache frequently accessed data in memory. They are ideal for caching
the results of expensive database queries or computationally intensive
operations. By caching the results, subsequent requests can be served from
the cache instead of querying the database or performing the operation
again, resulting in faster response times.

To use Redis or Memcached in your Laravel application, you first need to
install and configure the caching service on your server. Once installed, you
can configure Laravel to use the caching service by specifying the cache
driver in the **'config/cache.php'** configuration file.

For example, to use Redis as the cache driver, you would update the
'cache.php' configuration file as follows:

```
'default' => env('CACHE_DRIVER', 'redis'),

...

'redis' => [
    'client' => 'predis',
    'default' => [
        'host' => env('REDIS_HOST', '127.0.0.1'),
```

```php
        'password' => env('REDIS_PASSWORD', null),
        'port' => env('REDIS_PORT', 6379),
        'database' => 0,
    ],
],
```

This configuration specifies that Redis should be used as the cache driver, and sets the Redis connection details. You can then use Laravel's cache API to store and retrieve data from the cache. For example, to cache the result of a database query, you could do:

```php
$users = Cache::remember('users', $minutes, function () {
    return DB::table('users')->get();
});
```

This will cache the results of the **'users'** query for the specified number of minutes, and return the cached results if they exist. If the cache has expired or doesn't exist, the callback function will be called to retrieve the results from the database, and the results will be stored in the cache for future requests.

In addition to the built-in caching API, Laravel also provides a number of cache-related helper functions and features, such as cache tags, cache invalidation, and rate limiting. By using these features, you can further optimize your application's performance and reduce its database load.

11.2 Debugging and troubleshooting techniques

Debugging and troubleshooting are essential skills for maintaining Laravel applications. Here are some best practices to follow when debugging and troubleshooting:

1. Use the built-in debugging tools like Laravel Telescope and Laravel Debugbar to help you identify and fix issues.

Laravel provides several built-in debugging tools that can help you identify and fix issues in your application. Two of the most popular tools are Laravel Telescope and Laravel Debugbar.

Laravel Telescope is a powerful debugging tool that allows you to monitor your application's requests, exceptions, queries, and more in real-time. With Telescope, you can quickly identify performance bottlenecks and errors in your application. Telescope also provides a comprehensive dashboard that gives you a visual representation of your application's performance.

To use Telescope, you need to install it via Composer and then run the Telescope installation command:

```
composer require laravel/telescope
php artisan telescope:install
```

After installing Telescope, you can access the Telescope dashboard by visiting the **'/telescope'** route in your application.

Laravel Debugbar is another useful debugging tool that provides a visual representation of your application's performance and debugging information. Debugbar provides a toolbar that sits at the top of your application and displays various information about your application, such as the number of queries performed, the amount of memory used, and more.

To use Laravel Debugbar, you need to install it via Composer and then register the Debugbar service provider in your application's **'config/app.php'** file:

```
'providers' => [
    // Other service providers...

    Barryvdh\Debugbar\ServiceProvider::class,
],
```

After registering the Debugbar service provider, you can use the **'debugbar'** helper function to add debugging information to the Debugbar toolbar:

```
debugbar()->info('Hello, Debugbar!');
```

In addition to Laravel Telescope and Laravel Debugbar, Laravel also provides other debugging tools like error pages and logging that can help you identify and fix issues in your application.

2. Use error handling middleware to catch and handle exceptions before they cause issues in production.

Error handling middleware is an essential component of any production-level Laravel application. It allows you to catch and handle exceptions before they can cause issues in your application.

When an exception is thrown in your application, Laravel automatically looks for an exception handler to handle the exception. By default, Laravel provides a default exception handler that logs the exception and displays a generic error message to the user. However, this default behavior may not be sufficient for more complex applications.

To customize the way your application handles exceptions, you can create your own exception handler and register it with Laravel. This handler can then catch and handle exceptions in a way that is specific to your application.

In addition to a custom exception handler, you can also use error handling middleware to catch exceptions at the HTTP layer. Error handling middleware intercepts exceptions that are thrown during the handling of an HTTP request and allows you to handle them in a more granular way.

For example, you can use error handling middleware to catch and handle 404 errors or authentication errors before they reach your application code. This can help to reduce the likelihood of errors causing issues in production.

To create error handling middleware, you can use the **render** method in your middleware class. This method takes two parameters: the incoming request and the exception that was thrown. You can then use this method to catch and handle the exception in a way that is specific to your application.

Here is an example of error handling middleware that catches a specific type of exception and returns a custom response:

```php
<?php

namespace App\Http\Middleware;

use Illuminate\Http\Request;
use Closure;

class ExampleMiddleware
{
    public function handle(Request $request, Closure $next)
    {
        try {
            return $next($request);
        } catch (\Exception $exception) {
            if ($exception instanceof \App\Exceptions\CustomException) {
                return response()->json(['message' => 'Custom error message'], 500);
            }

            throw $exception;
```

```
        }
      }
    }
```

In this example, the middleware catches a specific type of exception
' (\App\Exceptions\CustomException)' and returns a custom JSON
response with a 500 status code. If the exception is not of the expected type,
it re-throws the exception to be handled by the default exception handler.

By using error handling middleware in your Laravel application, you can
catch and handle exceptions at the HTTP layer, providing a more granular
and specific approach to error handling.

3. Use logging to keep track of application events and errors.

Logging is an essential part of maintaining any application, as it allows
developers to keep track of application events and errors. Laravel provides
a powerful logging system that allows developers to log messages to various
channels, including files, the system error log, and third-party services like
Papertrail and Loggly.

To use the Laravel logging system, developers can use the **'Log'** facade,
which provides several static methods for logging messages at different
severity levels. For example, the following code logs a message at the **'info'**
level:

```
use Illuminate\Support\Facades\Log;

Log::info('User logged in', ['username' => $username]);
```

In this example, the **'info'** method is called on the **'Log'** facade, and the message "User logged in" is passed as the first argument. The second argument is an optional array of contextual data that can be used to provide additional information about the event being logged.

By default, Laravel logs messages to the **'storage/logs/laravel.log'** file. However, developers can configure the logging system to use different channels, such as the system error log or a third-party service. To configure the logging system, developers can modify the **'config/logging.php'** configuration file.

In addition to the built-in logging system, Laravel also provides several logging-related features, such as email notifications for critical errors and the ability to log messages to multiple channels simultaneously.

Using logging effectively can help developers identify and diagnose issues in their applications, as well as track application usage and performance over time. By logging messages at different severity levels and using contextual data to provide additional information, developers can gain valuable insights into their applications and ensure that they are running smoothly.

4. Monitor your application's performance and uptime using tools like New Relic or Datadog.

Monitoring your application's performance and uptime is crucial to ensure that your users have a positive experience and that your application is performing optimally. There are several tools available to help you monitor your application, including New Relic and Datadog.

New Relic is a cloud-based application performance monitoring tool that allows you to monitor your application's performance in real-time. It provides detailed information about your application's response times, throughput, error rates, and more. With New Relic, you can identify performance issues and bottlenecks and troubleshoot them quickly.

Datadog is another cloud-based monitoring tool that provides real-time monitoring and alerting for your applications. It allows you to monitor your application's performance and uptime, track requests and errors, and visualize your application's infrastructure. Datadog also provides integrations with other tools like Slack and PagerDuty, so you can receive alerts and notifications when issues arise.

In addition to using monitoring tools, it's important to establish performance baselines for your application and monitor metrics like response time and throughput regularly. This can help you identify trends and potential issues before they become critical.

It's also a good idea to set up alerts and notifications for key metrics, so you can be notified when performance issues arise. For example, you might set up an alert to notify you when the response time for a particular API endpoint exceeds a certain threshold.

By monitoring your application's performance and uptime, you can identify and resolve issues quickly, ensuring that your users have a positive experience and that your application is performing optimally.

5. Set up alerts to notify you of any issues or anomalies in your application.

Setting up alerts is a critical part of maintaining your Laravel application. Alerts can help you identify and address issues before they become major problems, and can ensure that your application is running smoothly and efficiently. Here are some steps to set up alerts for your Laravel application:

I. Identify key metrics: The first step in setting up alerts is to identify the key metrics that are most important to your application. This might include things like response time, server load, memory usage, and database performance.

II. Choose an alerting tool: There are many alerting tools available, including open-source options like Nagios and Icinga, as well as commercial solutions like PagerDuty and OpsGenie. Choose a tool that meets your needs and integrates well with your monitoring and logging tools.

III. Set up alerts: Once you've identified your key metrics and chosen an alerting tool, it's time to set up your alerts. This will typically involve configuring thresholds for each metric, so that you receive an alert when a metric exceeds a certain value. For example, you might set up an alert to notify you if response time exceeds 500ms.

IV. Configure notification channels: Alerts can be sent via email, SMS, Slack, or other channels. Configure your alerting tool to send alerts to the appropriate channels, and make sure that the right people are subscribed to each channel.

V. Test your alerts: Once you've set up your alerts and notification channels, it's important to test them to make sure they're working correctly. Create some test scenarios that will trigger your alerts, and verify that you receive the alerts via your chosen notification channels.

VI. Monitor and refine: Once your alerts are up and running, it's important to monitor them regularly to ensure that they're still relevant and effective. Refine your alerts as needed based on changes to your application or infrastructure, and make sure that they continue to provide value over time.

By setting up alerts for your Laravel application, you can ensure that you're notified of any issues or anomalies as soon as they occur, and take action to address them before they become major problems. This can help you maintain a high level of performance and uptime for your application, and provide a better experience for your users.

11.3 Best practices for maintaining Laravel applications

Maintaining a Laravel application requires ongoing attention and effort. Here are some best practices to follow to ensure that your application remains secure and performant:

1. Keep your dependencies up-to-date by regularly updating to the latest versions of Laravel and its components.

Keeping your dependencies up-to-date is crucial for the security and stability of your Laravel application. Regularly updating to the latest versions of Laravel and its components ensures that you have access to the latest security patches, bug fixes, and performance improvements.

To keep your dependencies up-to-date, you can use Composer, the package manager for PHP. Composer allows you to manage the dependencies of your application, including Laravel and its components, by specifying them in a **'composer.json'** file. To update your dependencies, you can run the following command:

```
composer update
```

This command will update all the dependencies specified in your **'composer.json'** file to their latest versions. However, you should be careful when updating your dependencies, as updates may introduce breaking changes or compatibility issues with your application.

2. Use automated testing to ensure that your application continues to function correctly as you make changes.

Automated testing is an important aspect of maintaining a stable and reliable application. Laravel provides a built-in testing framework, PHPUnit, which makes it easy to write and run tests for your application.

To get started with testing in Laravel, you can create test classes for your controllers, models, and other components. These test classes typically extend the PHPUnit TestCase class and contain test methods that use assertions to verify that the expected behavior is being exhibited by the code.

For example, if you have a controller method that should return a view with a specific title, you can write a test method that makes a request to the controller and asserts that the response contains the expected title. This ensures that the controller is functioning as intended and that any changes made to the code in the future do not break this behavior.

In addition to unit testing, Laravel also provides tools for feature testing, which involves testing the behavior of your application as a user would experience it. Feature tests typically involve simulating user interactions with your application, such as filling out forms and clicking buttons, and then asserting that the expected behavior occurs.

To ensure that your tests run automatically whenever changes are made to your codebase, you can set up a continuous integration (CI) pipeline using a tool like Travis CI or CircleCI. This pipeline will automatically build and test your application whenever changes are pushed to your repository, allowing you to catch any issues early on.

By using automated testing, you can ensure that your application continues to function correctly as you make changes, and catch any issues before they reach production. This can save you time and effort in the long run, as well as provide peace of mind that your application is functioning as intended.

3. Regularly review and update your security measures, including password policies and two-factor authentication.

Regularly reviewing and updating your security measures is crucial for maintaining the security of your Laravel application. Here are some ways to do it:

I. Password Policies: Make sure you have a strong password policy in place for your application. Encourage your users to use complex passwords and regularly change them. You can also use tools like password managers to help your users create and store strong passwords.

II. Two-Factor Authentication: Enabling two-factor authentication (2FA) adds an extra layer of security to your application. It requires users to enter a second form of identification, such as a code sent to their phone or an authenticator app, in addition to their password. Laravel has built-in support for 2FA.

III. Regular Security Audits: Performing regular security audits can help identify potential vulnerabilities in your application. You can use tools like security scanners or penetration testing services to identify security issues and address them before they can be exploited.

IV. Keep Up-to-date with Laravel Security Updates: Laravel has a dedicated security team that regularly releases security patches and updates. Stay up-to-date with these updates to ensure that your application is protected from the latest security threats.

V. Secure Your Database: Make sure that your database is secured and that access to sensitive data is restricted. Use strong passwords and encryption to protect your data. You can also use tools like database firewalls to help secure your database.

VI. Implement Rate Limiting: Rate limiting helps prevent brute force attacks by limiting the number of requests that can be made within a certain timeframe. You can use Laravel's built-in rate limiting middleware or implement a third-party package to add rate limiting to your application.

By regularly reviewing and updating your security measures, you can help protect your Laravel application from potential threats and ensure that your users' data is secure.

4. Implement a process for handling security vulnerabilities and applying security patches.

Implementing a process for handling security vulnerabilities and applying security patches is a critical part of maintaining the security of your Laravel application. Here are some key steps to follow:

I. Stay informed about security vulnerabilities: Keep yourself up-to-date with the latest security threats and vulnerabilities affecting Laravel and its dependencies. This can be done by subscribing to security mailing lists, following security blogs, and participating in security forums.

II. Evaluate the impact of vulnerabilities: When you become aware of a vulnerability, assess the risk it poses to your application. Determine which components of your application are affected and the likelihood and potential impact of an attack.

III. Apply security patches promptly: Laravel regularly releases security patches to address known vulnerabilities. When a patch is released, apply it promptly to ensure that your application is not vulnerable to the associated threat.

IV. Implement secure coding practices: Adopt secure coding practices when developing your application to minimize the likelihood of introducing vulnerabilities. This includes using input validation and output encoding, avoiding the use of eval(), and using strong encryption.

V. Conduct regular security audits: Conduct regular security audits to identify vulnerabilities in your application. This can be done manually or using automated tools. Address any identified vulnerabilities promptly.

VI. Have a plan for responding to security incidents: Develop a plan for responding to security incidents, including how to isolate and contain an attack, notify users, and restore services.

VII. Train your team: Ensure that your development team is trained in secure coding practices and understands the importance of maintaining the security of your application.

By following these steps, you can ensure that your Laravel application remains secure and protected from potential security threats.

5. Document your code and processes to make it easier for other developers to work with your application.

Documenting code and processes is an essential aspect of software development that can help improve the maintainability and scalability of an application. Here are some ways to document your Laravel code and processes:

I. Document your code with comments: Add comments to your code to explain what it does and how it works. This can be helpful for other developers who need to understand your codebase.

II. Use inline documentation: Inline documentation is similar to comments, but it follows a specific format that makes it easier to generate documentation automatically. Tools like PHPDocumentor can generate API documentation from inline documentation.

III. Write README files: A README file is a document that explains how to install and use your application. It can also contain information about the project's goals, architecture, and development process.

IV. Use version control: Version control tools like Git can help you track changes to your code and documentation over time. This makes it easier to collaborate with other developers and roll back changes if necessary.

V. Create user manuals: If you're building a web application, create user manuals or help files to explain how to use the application. This can be especially helpful for non-technical users who may not be familiar with web applications.

VI. Use a wiki: A wiki is a collaborative tool that can be used to document code, processes, and other aspects of your project. This can be especially helpful for large teams that need to share information and collaborate on documentation.

VII. Conduct code reviews: Code reviews are a process where other developers review your code to identify potential issues or improvements. Code reviews can help ensure that your code is maintainable and follows best practices.

By documenting your code and processes, you can make it easier for other developers to work with your application and ensure that it remains maintainable and scalable over time.

By following these best practices for deployment and maintenance, you can ensure that your Laravel application remains secure, performant, and reliable over time.

Chapter 12: Testing in Laravel with PHPUnit

Testing is an essential part of any software development process, and Laravel provides built-in support for testing with PHPUnit. PHPUnit is a widely used testing framework for PHP, and Laravel integrates seamlessly with it, making it easy to write and run tests for your Laravel application.

In this chapter, we will cover the basics of testing in Laravel with PHPUnit, including how to set up your testing environment, write and run tests, and use Laravel's built-in testing tools.

12.1 Setting Up Your Testing Environment

To get started with testing in Laravel, you will need to set up a testing environment. Laravel provides a convenient way to do this using the Artisan command-line tool. To create a new testing environment, simply run the following command:

```
php artisan make:test MyTest
```

This will create a new test file named **'MyTest.php'** in the **'tests'** directory of your Laravel project. You can then add your tests to this file.

12.2 Writing Tests

Tests in Laravel are written using PHPUnit, and follow a simple structure. Each test should extend the **'TestCase'** class provided by Laravel, and should have one or more methods that test a specific feature of your application.

For example, let's say we want to test that a user can be created and stored in the database. We could write a test like this:

```php
class UserTest extends TestCase
{
    public function testCreateUser()
    {
        $user = factory(User::class)->create([
            'name' => 'John Doe',
            'email' => 'john@example.com',
            'password' => bcrypt('password')
        ]);

        $this->assertEquals('John Doe', $user->name);
        $this->assertEquals('john@example.com', $user->email);
    }
}
```

This test creates a new user using Laravel's factory, sets the user's name, email, and password, and then checks that the user was created with the correct values.

12.3 Running Tests

To run your tests, simply run the following command:

```
vendor/bin/phpunit
```

This will run all of the tests in your Laravel application. You can also run a specific test by specifying the path to the test file or directory:

```
vendor/bin/phpunit tests/MyTest.php
```

12.4 Using Laravel's Built-In Testing Tools

Laravel provides a range of testing tools to make it easier to write and run tests. Some of these tools include:

- Factories: Laravel's factory classes make it easy to generate fake data for your tests. This can be especially useful when testing database interactions.

- Assertions: Laravel provides a range of built-in assertions that you can use to test your application. These include assertions for checking that a value is equal to another value, that an array contains a specific value, and more.

- Mocking: Laravel's mocking library allows you to create mock objects to use in your tests. This can be useful when testing code that interacts with external services or APIs.

Testing is an essential part of any software development process, and Laravel makes it easy to write and run tests using PHPUnit. By setting up your testing environment, writing tests, and using Laravel's built-in testing tools, you can ensure that your Laravel application is reliable, secure, and performs as expected.

Chapter13 : Advanced Eloquent

Laravel's Eloquent ORM is a powerful tool for working with databases in PHP. In addition to basic CRUD operations, Eloquent provides advanced features such as relationships, eager loading, and database transactions. In this chapter, we'll explore these advanced features and how to use them effectively in your Laravel application.

13.1 Relationships

One of the most powerful features of Eloquent is its ability to handle relationships between database tables. Eloquent supports several types of relationships, including:

- One-to-One

- One-to-Many

- Many-to-Many

- Has-Many-Through

- Polymorphic Relationships

Let's take a look at each of these relationship types and how to define them in Eloquent.

13.1.1 One-to-One Relationship

A one-to-one relationship is a relationship where each record in one table is associated with one and only one record in another table. For example, a user may have one profile.

To define a one-to-one relationship in Eloquent, we need to define a method on the parent model that returns a **'hasOne'** relationship. Here's an example:

```
class User extends Model
{
    public function profile()
    {
        return $this->hasOne(Profile::class);
    }
}
```

In this example, we have defined a **'profile'** method on the **'User'** model that returns a **'hasOne'** relationship. The **'Profile'** model is passed as the first argument to the **'hasOne'** method, which tells Eloquent that the **'User'** model has a one-to-one relationship with the **'Profile'** model.

To access the related **'Profile'** model, we can simply call the **'profile'** method on a **'User'** model:

```
$user = User::find(1);

$profile = $user->profile;
```

13.1.2 One-to-Many Relationship

A one-to-many relationship is a relationship where each record in one table can be associated with one or many records in another table. For example, a user may have many posts.

To define a one-to-many relationship in Eloquent, we need to define a method on the parent model that returns a **'hasMany'** relationship. Here's an example:

```
class User extends Model
{
  public function posts()
  {
    return $this->hasMany(Post::class);
  }
}
```

In this example, we have defined a **'posts'** method on the **'User'** model that returns a **'hasMany'** relationship. The **'Post'** model is passed as the first argument to the **'hasMany'** method, which tells Eloquent that the **'User'** model has a one-to-many relationship with the **'Post'** model.

To access the related **'Post'** models, we can simply call the **'posts'** method on a **'User'** model:

```
$user = User::find(1);

$posts = $user->posts;
```

13.1.3 Many-to-Many Relationship

A many-to-many relationship is a relationship where each record in one table can be associated with many records in another table, and vice versa. For example, a user may belong to many roles, and a role may be assigned to many users.

To define a many-to-many relationship in Eloquent, we need to define a method on both the parent model and the related model that returns a **'belongsToMany'** relationship. Here's an example:

```php
class User extends Model
{
    public function roles()
    {
        return $this->belongsToMany(Role::class);
    }
}


class Role extends Model
{
```

```php
    public function users()
    {
        return $this->belongsToMany(User::class);
    }
}
```

In this example, we have defined a **'roles'** method on the **'User'** model and a **users** method on the **'Role'** model to establish a many-to-many relationship between users and roles.

```php
    class User extends Model
    {
        public function roles()
        {
            return $this->belongsToMany(Role::class);
        }
    }


    class Role extends Model
    {
        public function users()
        {
            return $this->belongsToMany(User::class);
        }
    }
```

With this setup, we can easily access the roles that belong to a user and the users that belong to a role.

To retrieve all the roles for a user, we can simply call the **'roles'** method on the user instance:

    $user = User::find(1);

    $roles = $user->roles;

This will return a collection of **'Role'** models associated with the user. Similarly, we can retrieve all the users for a role by calling the **'users'** method on a **'Role'** instance:

    $role = Role::find(1);

    $users = $role->users;

This will return a collection of **'User'** models associated with the role.
We can also add or remove roles from a user by calling the **'attach'** and **'detach'** methods on the **'roles'** relationship:

```
$user = User::find(1);

$user->roles()->attach($roleId);

$user->roles()->detach($roleId);
```

In this example, **'$roleId'** is the ID of the role we want to attach or detach. We can also pass an array of role IDs to the **'attach'** method to attach multiple roles at once:

```
$user->roles()->attach([$roleId1, $roleId2, $roleId3]);
```

Eloquent also provides other methods for working with many-to-many relationships, such as **'sync'**, **'syncWithoutDetaching'**, and **'toggle'**. These methods provide additional flexibility for managing many-to-many relationships in your Laravel application.

Chapter 14: Queues and Jobs

Laravel's queues and jobs provide a powerful system for handling long-running tasks in the background of your application. This chapter will cover the basics of queues and jobs, how to set up a queue system, how to create and dispatch jobs, and how to monitor and manage your queues.

14.1 Queues Overview

Queues are a way of processing tasks asynchronously in the background of your application. A task can be anything from sending an email, processing an image, or performing a complex database query. Queues help to prevent these tasks from blocking the main thread of your application and improve performance and scalability.

In Laravel, queues are managed by a driver system. Laravel provides several built-in drivers such as Redis, Beanstalkd, and Amazon SQS, as well as the ability to use custom drivers. Each driver has its own configuration and requirements, but the basic queue workflow remains the same.

14.2 Setting up a Queue System

To set up a queue system, you must first configure the driver in the **'config/queue.php'** file. Laravel provides configurations for several drivers, including Redis, Beanstalkd, and Amazon SQS. Once the driver is configured, you can start the queue worker process using the **'php artisan queue:work'** command.

14.3 Creating and Dispatching Jobs

A job is a unit of work that can be queued and processed by the queue worker. Jobs are typically defined as classes that implement the **'Illuminate\Contracts\Queue\ShouldQueue'** interface. When a job is dispatched, it is added to the queue and processed by the next available worker.

To create a job, you can use the **'php artisan make:job'** command to generate a new job class. Inside the job class, you can define the work that needs to be performed. For example, a job that sends an email might look like this:

```php
use Illuminate\Bus\Queueable;
use Illuminate\Contracts\Queue\ShouldQueue;
use Illuminate\Foundation\Bus\Dispatchable;
use Illuminate\Queue\InteractsWithQueue;
use Illuminate\Queue\SerializesModels;

class SendEmail implements ShouldQueue
{
    use Dispatchable, InteractsWithQueue, Queueable, SerializesModels;

    protected $user;
```

```php
public function __construct($user)
{
    $this->user = $user;
}


public function handle()
{
    // Send email logic here
}
}
```

To dispatch the job, you can use the **'dispatch'** method on the job class:

```php
$user = User::find(1);

SendEmail::dispatch($user);
```

This will add the job to the queue and process it when the next available worker is ready.

14.4 Monitoring and Managing Queues

Laravel provides several useful tools for monitoring and managing your queues. The **'php artisan queue:listen'** command allows you to monitor the queue and process jobs as they are added. You can also use the **'php artisan queue:work'** command to start a dedicated worker process that will process jobs continuously.

Laravel also provides a dashboard for monitoring and managing queues called Horizon. Horizon provides real-time monitoring of your queues, detailed job metrics, and the ability to retry or delete failed jobs.

Chapter summary

Using queues and jobs in Laravel can greatly improve the performance and scalability of your application. By offloading long-running tasks to the background, you can prevent these tasks from blocking the main thread of your application and improve the overall user experience.

Chapter 15: Deployment with Docker

Deploying Laravel applications with Docker has become a popular option for many developers due to its ease of use and ability to provide a consistent and portable deployment environment. In this chapter, we will cover the basics of Docker and how to use Docker to deploy Laravel applications.

15.1 What is Docker?

Docker is an open-source platform that allows developers to easily create, deploy, and run applications in a containerized environment. Containers are lightweight, portable, and isolated environments that contain all the necessary dependencies and configuration required to run an application.

Docker containers can be easily created, distributed, and deployed across different operating systems and cloud providers, making it an ideal solution for deploying applications in different environments.

15.2 Docker Basics

Before we dive into deploying a Laravel application with Docker, let's cover some Docker basics.

15.2.1 Dockerfile

A Dockerfile is a text file that contains instructions on how to build a Docker image. A Docker image is a static snapshot of a container that can be used to create multiple instances of the same container.

The Dockerfile contains instructions on how to build the container image, such as installing dependencies, configuring the environment, and running the application.

Here is an example of a Dockerfile for a Laravel application:

```
# Base image
FROM php:7.4-fpm-alpine

# Install dependencies
RUN apk update && \
  apk add --no-cache --virtual .build-deps \
    $PHPIZE_DEPS \
    curl \
    libpng-dev \
    libjpeg-turbo-dev \
    freetype-dev \
    libzip-dev \
    postgresql-dev \
  && apk add --no-cache \
    libpng \
    libjpeg-turbo \
    freetype \
    libzip \
    postgresql-client \
  && docker-php-ext-install \
    pdo_mysql \
```

```dockerfile
    pdo_pgsql \
    gd \
    zip \
  && pecl install \
    redis \
    xdebug \
  && docker-php-ext-enable \
    redis \
    xdebug \
  && apk del .build-deps

# Copy application files
COPY . /var/www/html

# Set working directory
WORKDIR /var/www/html

# Expose port
EXPOSE 9000

# Start server
CMD ["php-fpm"]
```

This Dockerfile installs the necessary dependencies, copies the application files to the container, sets the working directory, and starts the PHP-FPM server.

15.2.2 Docker Compose

Docker Compose is a tool for defining and running multi-container Docker applications. It allows you to define all the services required to run your application, such as the application server, database, and cache, in a single YAML file.

Here is an example of a Docker Compose file for a Laravel application:

```yaml
version: '3'
services:
  app:
    build:
      context: .
      dockerfile: Dockerfile
    ports:
      - 8000:9000
    volumes:
      - .:/var/www/html
    environment:
      DB_HOST: db
      DB_PORT: 5432
      DB_DATABASE: myapp
```

      DB_USERNAME: myuser
      DB_PASSWORD: mypassword
  db:
    image: postgres:13-alpine
    environment:
      POSTGRES_DB: myapp
      POSTGRES_USER: myuser
      POSTGRES_PASSWORD: mypassword

This Docker Compose file defines two services: the application server and the database. The application server is built using the Dockerfile defined in the current directory and exposed on port 8000. The database is using the official Postgres Docker image and configured with the necessary environment variables.

15.2 3 Docker Registry

A Docker Registry is a server-side application that stores and manages Docker images. It serves as a central repository where Docker images can be stored and distributed to different Docker hosts or environments.

A Docker Registry can be used to host both public and private Docker images, allowing teams to share and distribute their images across different environments and platforms. It also provides access control and authentication mechanisms to ensure that only authorized users have access to sensitive or proprietary images.

There are several options for hosting a Docker Registry, including Docker Hub (a public registry maintained by Docker), private cloud-based solutions such as Amazon Elastic Container Registry (ECR) and Google Container Registry (GCR), and self-hosted solutions such as Docker Registry and Harbor.

Using a Docker Registry can simplify the deployment process of Dockerized applications, as images can be easily pulled from the registry and deployed to any environment. It also enables version control and traceability, allowing teams to easily manage and track changes to their images over time.

Chapter 16: References and further reading

Recommended books and articles for further reading on Laravel

Books:

- "Laravel: Up & Running" by Matt Stauffer

- "Laravel 8 Application Development Cookbook" by Rangavasan N

- "Mastering Laravel" by Christopher John Pecoraro

Articles:

- "Laravel Documentation" - Official Laravel documentation covering all aspects of the framework

- "How to Build a Laravel Application from Scratch" by Povilas Korop - A step-by-step guide to building a Laravel application

- "Best Practices for Laravel Applications" by Taylor Otwell - Tips and advice from the creator of Laravel on how to build high-quality Laravel applications

- "Using Docker for Laravel Development and Deployment" by Dries Vints - A detailed guide on how to use Docker to develop and deploy Laravel applications

Appendix A

Setting up a deployment script is an essential part of using a deployment tool like Capistrano or Deployer to automate the deployment process of your Laravel application. Here's how you can create a deployment script that defines the steps to be taken during the deployment process:

1. Identify the steps involved in the deployment process: Before you can create a deployment script, you need to identify the steps involved in deploying your Laravel application. These may include running database migrations, clearing caches, uploading code files, and restarting servers.

2. Create a deployment configuration file: Next, create a deployment configuration file that specifies the servers and settings for your application. This file typically includes server IP addresses, SSH user names, and passwords.

3. Define the deployment tasks: Once you have identified the steps involved in the deployment process, you can create a series of tasks that correspond to each step. For example, you may create a task to run database migrations or clear caches.

4. Write the deployment script: Using a deployment tool like Capistrano or Deployer, you can write a deployment script that defines the tasks to be executed during the deployment process. This script typically includes the configuration file, a list of servers to deploy to, and the deployment tasks.

5. Test the deployment script: Before deploying your application, it's important to test your deployment script in a staging environment to ensure that it works as expected. This will help you catch any errors or issues before deploying to production.

6. Deploy your application: Once you have tested your deployment script and verified that it works as expected, you can deploy your application to your production environment using the deployment tool.

By following these steps, you can create a deployment script that defines the steps to be taken during the deployment process of your Laravel application. This can help automate the deployment process, save time, and reduce the risk of errors and inconsistencies across environments.

Example of creating a deployment script for a Laravel application using Deployer:

1. Install Deployer: First, install Deployer by running the following command in your Laravel application directory:

   composer require deployer/deployer --dev

2. Create a Deployer configuration file: Create a **'deploy.php'** file in the root directory of your Laravel application and add the following code:

```php
<?php

require 'recipe/common.php';

// Set the repository URL
set('repository', 'git@github.com:yourusername/your-repo.git');

// Set the deployment path on the server
set('deploy_path', '~/your-project');

// Define the tasks to run during deployment
task('deploy', [
    'deploy:prepare',
    'deploy:lock',
    'deploy:release',
    'deploy:update_code',
    'deploy:shared',
    'deploy:writable',
    'deploy:clear_paths',
    'deploy:symlink',
    'deploy:unlock',
    'cleanup',
])->desc('Deploy your Laravel application');
```

```php
// Set the server configuration
host('your-server-ip')
    ->user('your-ssh-username')
    ->set('deploy_path', '~/your-project');

// Set the SSH identity file
set('ssh_type', 'native');
set('ssh_multiplexing', false);
set('ssh_identity_file', '/path/to/your/private/key');

// Set the Git branch to deploy
set('branch', 'master');
```

This configuration file sets the repository URL, deployment path, and defines the tasks to run during deployment. It also sets the server configuration and SSH identity file.

3. Define the deployment tasks: In the same **'deploy.php'** file, add the following tasks to define the steps to be taken during the deployment process:

```php
task('artisan:migrate', function () {
    run('{{bin/php}} {{release_path}}/artisan migrate');
})->desc('Run database migrations');
```

```php
task('artisan:cache:clear', function () {
    run('{{bin/php}} {{release_path}}/artisan cache:clear');
})->desc('Clear the application cache');

task('artisan:config:cache', function () {
    run('{{bin/php}} {{release_path}}/artisan config:cache');
})->desc('Cache the configuration files');

task('artisan:view:clear', function () {
    run('{{bin/php}} {{release_path}}/artisan view:clear');
})->desc('Clear the compiled view files');
```

These tasks use the **'run'** command to execute Laravel's **'artisan'** command to run database migrations, clear the application cache, cache the configuration files, and clear the compiled view files.

4. Test the deployment script: Before deploying your application, test your deployment script by running the following command in your Laravel application directory:

```
dep deploy
```

This command will run the deployment script and execute the defined tasks.

5. Deploy your application: Once you have tested your deployment script and verified that it works as expected, you can deploy your application to your production environment by running the following command:

   dep deploy production

This command will deploy your application to the server specified in the configuration file.

By following these steps, you can create a deployment script that defines the steps to be taken during the deployment process of your Laravel application using Deployer.